Sigurgeir Sigurjónsson

Iceland small world

D0408600

PORTFOLIO

Look...

Foreword by Arni Thorarinsson

"Look," my father said. "Look at the lava."

What's there to see? It's just lava, I thought, and returned to reading The Island of Adventure by Enid Blyton, my first influence in crime fiction writing.

What is the big deal? Endless endless lava, endless moss. Endless wilderness.

It could have been Skaftáreldahraun (page 248-249). "And this is where it comes from," my mother added, pointing through the window at some mountains in the distance. "Look at the volcanoes."

It was tough to read a book in the backseat of the family's old Oldsmobile. The roads were like washboards in those days. I looked through the cloud of dust drifting over the landscape, my little sister sleeping beside me.

"Where can we buy a hot dog?" I asked. "There's nothing here."

"Look at the sheep," my mother said as the road ran past some green farmland with flocks of sheep dispersing and grouping together, like people without leadership.

They reminded me of hot dogs running around, searching for mustard and ketchup.

"Look at this volcanic lake. Feel the peace and quiet. And it's a great place to catch some Salmo trutta," said my father.

It could have been Ljótipollur (Ugly Puddle) in Landmannalaugar (page 84-85).

Salmo trutta? Give me a hamburger and French fries.

Boring, boring.

"When do we get back to Reykjavík? I would like to watch some television."

"Just look at that swimming pool. Hot water straight from the earth. To bathe in and swim in. Isn't that a miracle?"

It could not have been the new pool in Hofsós (page 18-19). It wasn't there in 1960.

A miracle? Hot water? What's so special about that? We have lots of it in Reykjavík as well. We just turn on the tap.

Driving on. Boring, boring.

"Look at that solitary man on the glacier."

It could have been Svínafellsjökull (page 60-61).

"Listen to the silence."

"You're joking. Why can't we rather go to Costa del Sol?"

"Look at the old farmhouse."

Yes, it's quite ugly. No wonder the people have left and moved to the city.

It could have been in Melrakkaslétta. Except they are rebuilding it for a brave new world.

Let's have some rock and roll on the radio.

And then the giants wake up. The rock and roll is coming straight at us as they spew fire and brimstone. At that moment we see.

It could be the volcanic eruption in Fimmvörðuháls (page 87). When the beautiful sound of silence is broken and nature screams at us we have to take notice.

The island of adventure was right in front of me. It was too close to see and sense its magic. It was home. And still is.

Look. And see.

Skaftáreldahraun (The lava field from Laki Fires) Erupted in 1783.
Morsárdalur valley, Skaftafell National Park.

Skógafoss waterfall frozen in ice.

The glacial lake Jökulsárlón south of Vatnajökull glacier.

The glacier Svínafellsjökull east of Skaftafell. South Iceland.
Right page. Skaftafell National Park.

The small village Hofsós in Skagafjörður fjord.

The swimming pool in Hofsós village, right by the sea.

The abandoned farm Skipalón on Melrakkaslétta plain,
one of the northernmost settlements in Iceland.
Inside and outside the house.

Mælifellssandur plain north of Mýrdalsjökull glacier.

Jökulgilsá river near Landmannalaugar.

A pile of driftwood in the northernmost part of Iceland.
The sea stack Vondiklettur by Álftafjörður fjord in East Iceland.

Möðrudalur farm in northeast Iceland. Herðubreið mountain in the background.

Sheep gathering in Mývatnssveit.

View to the east from Dyrhólaey promontory.
The beach in Landeyjar region in South Iceland.

The waterfall Gullfoss.

Dettifoss, the most powerful waterfall in Europe. Jökulsárgljúfur National Park.

Gullfoss waterfall frozen in ice in the middle of December.
Left page. Strokkur, a geyser in the Geysir area.

The broad shore at Rauðisandur (Red Sand) in the Westfjords.

Seals are a common sight on Jökulsárlón glacial lake, especially in winter.

In the Kerlingarfjöll range in the central highlands lie Hveradalir valleys, a hot spring area with countless fumaroles.

Möðrudalur farm lies deep in the uplands of northeast Iceland.

47

A small waterflow falls from a mossy cliff in the canyon Gjáin.
Aldeyjarfoss waterfall, in the innermost part of Bárðardalur valley,
surrounded by basalt columns.

The lighthouse on Dyrhólaey promontory.

Seljalandsfoss waterfall in winter.

Blooming lupines by Route 1 in South Iceland.

In spring 2010, a large eruption occurred in Eyjafjallajökull glacier.

In March 2010, an eruption began on Fimmvörðuháls mountain ridge, one of Iceland's most popular hiking routes. This was a precursor to a larger eruption nearby which occurred in Eyjafjallajökull glacier.

A mountain guide explores Svínafellsjökull glacier.

Jökulsárlón glacial lake south of Vatnajökull glacier.

Ice floes on the beach outside of Jökulsárlón glacial lake.
A fireworks display by Jökulsárlón glacial lake.

Tourists by the glacial lake Jökulsárlón.

The December sun at Jökulsárlón glacial lake.

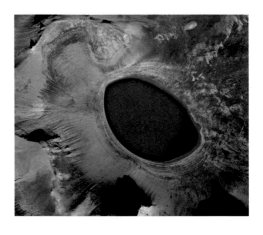

Sauðafellsvatn lake north of Hekla volcano.
The explosion crater Víti by the caldera Askja. The water temperature
is suitable for bathing.

Reynisdrangar sea stacks by the village Vík í Mýrdal.

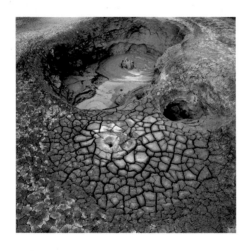

Mud pool east of Lake Mývatn in North Iceland.
Hveradalir valleys in the Kerlingarfjöll range, central highlands.

Abandoned settlement on Melrakkaslétta plain in the northernmost part of Iceland.

Goðafoss waterfall in Skjálfandafljót river.

Sunset by the south coast.
Summer by Jökulsárlón glacial lake. The lake continually changes
with the seasons.

Dyrhólaey promontory in twilight.

The explosion crater Ljótipollur, a short way from Landmannalaugar.

Eruption on Fimmvörðuháls mountain ridge.
The highlands to the north are visible in the distance.

During the summer, thousands of swans stay in Lónsfjörður fjord in southeast Iceland.

Dynjandi waterfall in Arnarfjörður fjord in the Westfjords.

The camping site at Landmannalaugar in Iceland's central highlands.
A hot pool in Landmannalaugar.

Climbers on Svínafellsjökull glacier.

Basalt columns in Reynisfjara beach in South Iceland.

Craters in the central highlands, a short way from Veiðivötn lakes.
There is good trout fishing in Veiðivötn lakes.

The waterfall Seljalandsfoss, at the roots of Eyjafjöll mountains in South Iceland.

Skaftáreldahraun lava field in South Iceland. From the eruption in 1783.

Gjáin, a canyon in Þjórsárdalur valley in South Iceland.
Left page. Dense spray rises from the canyon by Gullfoss waterfall.

By the mountain Brennisteinsalda in Landmannalaugar.

The Icelandic horse is a comfortable and smooth riding horse.
In its time, the mare Nös, on the right, was one of the greatest riding
horses in Iceland.

An abandoned farm in the northernmost part of Iceland.

Ásbyrgi canyon, in the northernmost part of the National Park.

An iceberg on Fjallsárlón, a glacial lake south of Vatnajökull.
Left page. The view over Jökulsárlón glacial lake.

Hikers on Svínafellsjökull glacier.

There is a large gannet colony on Langanes peninsula.

Razorbills, a colonial seabird.

Puffins are common birds in Iceland.

Látrabjarg, Westfjords.

The aggressive Arctic Terns over Drangar in the Strandir region, northwest Iceland.

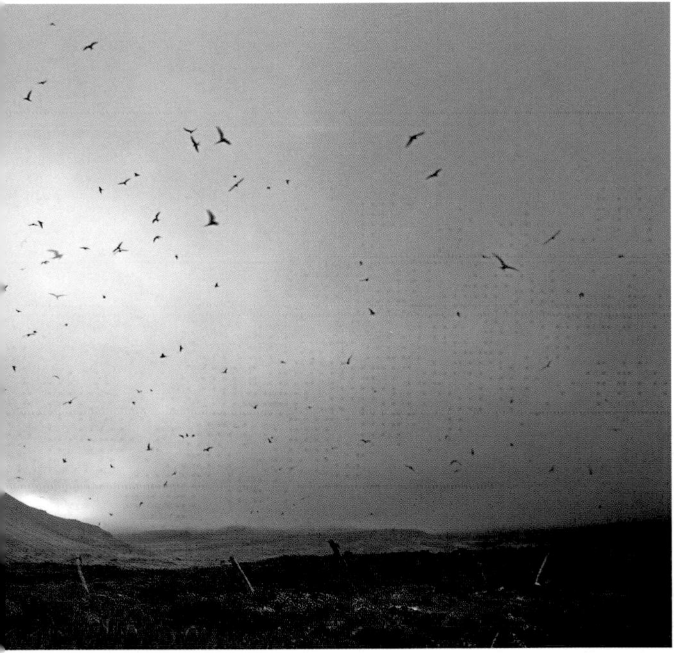

By the glacial lake Jökulsárlón.
Left page. An iceberg on Fjallsárlón glacial lake.

Bubbling mud pools east of Lake Mývatn.

An iceberg on Fjallsárlón glacial lake.

Álfakirkjan (The Elf Church) in Jökulsárgljúfur National Park.
Right page. Hljóðaklettar (Echo Rocks), basalt columns in the same canyon.

Dyrhólaey promontory with Eyjafjallajökull glacier in the background.

The lake Langisjór west of Vatnajökull glacier.

Old lava in the highlands north of Mýrdalsjökull glacier.
Left page. The Skagafjörður Heritage Museum at Glaumbær in North Iceland.

Puffin colony in Mánáreyjar islands.

Camping site by the cabin in Landmannalaugar.

The peak Þumall in Skaftafellsfjöll mountains in South Iceland.
Seals lie by a hole in the ice at Jökulsárlón glacial lake in winter.

The Skógar Folk Museum at the roots of Eyjafjöll mountains.

The ground covered with volcanic ash by the old swimming pool Seljavallalaug.

147

The canyons below Dettifoss waterfall. Jökulsárgljúfur National Park.
Skógafoss waterfall at the roots of Eyjafjöll mountains. A glittering ice palace
in early March.

Dynkur waterfall in the upper part of Þjórsá river.

Barren uplands surround the remote farm Möðrudalur.

In Skaftafell National Park. The waterfall Svartifoss.
Left page. The view to Öræfajökull, the highest mountain in the country.

There is diverse birdlife by Lake Mývatn in North Iceland.

By the hamlet Hellnar on the west part of Snæfellsnes peninsula.

There are numerous bubbling mud pools east of Lake Mývatn.
Dettifoss. The picture is taken west of the waterfall during heavy winds.

Lónbjörg, Snæfellsnes peninsula.

A lot of driftwood washes up on the northernmost shores of Iceland.

Hvalnes church, built in 1887, Reykjanes peninsula.
Graffity on ruins, close to Hvalnes church.

A small geothermal power station by Lake Mývatn.

Geothermal area in the highlands north of Mýrdalsjökull glacier.

Basalt columns by Kálfshamarsvík inlet in northwest Iceland.
Diverse columnar basalt formations characterise Kálfshamarsvík.

Veiðivötn is a cluster of lakes in the highlands.

175

Jökulsárlón glacial lake on a cold winter's day.

Fumarole in the hot spring area east of Lake Mývatn.

The eruption on Fimmvörðuháls mountain ridge in spring 2010. A view of the eruptive fissure from north to south.

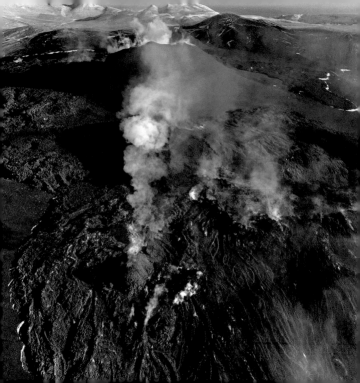

An old farmhouse at Grænavatn homestead by Lake Mývatn.

The mountain Háalda by Landmannalaugar.

Old cairns along the highland track up to Veiðivötn lakes.
Left page. Basalt columns in Reynisfjara beach near Dyrhólaey.

Reykjadalir, a hot spring area in the highlands.

Herðubreið mountain towers over the uplands in northeast Iceland.

189

Lava column by Lake Mývatn.

Dverghamrar, columnar basalt pillars in South Iceland.

Raufarhöfn village is the northernmost locality in Iceland.

Only about 200 people live in Raufarhöfn village today.

The explosion crater Ljótipollur near Landmannalaugar. It is easy to walk around the lake along the crater rim.

Grindavík, on Reykjanes peninsula, is among the major fishing towns in Iceland.

A pond by Tungnaá river which flows to the west from Vatnajökull glacier.

A skerry in Kálfshamarsvík, a columnar basalt inlet in northwest Iceland.
Geese in flight over Kálfshamarsvík inlet.

By Arnarfjörður fjord in the Westfjords. The shore is covered with shell sand.

Landmannalaugar are hot springs in the central highlands.

Horse farming and horsemanship are popular in Iceland. Horses can therefore be seen grazing around the country.

Arctic River Beauty growing in a small oasis. Herðubreið mountain in the background.

The father and son at Ós near the innermost part of Arnarfjörður.

A track from North Iceland south to the highlands by Vatnajökull glacier.

Skaftafell National Park.

Svínafellsjökull glacier east of Skaftafell National Park.

There is unusually diverse landscape in the highlands north of Mýrdalsjökull glacier: mountains and wetlands, lava fields, and geothermal areas.

Hekla volcano rises over the countryside of South Iceland.

The mountain Hestfjall in Ísafjarðardjúp bay in the Westfjords.

The Icelandic horse is a good-natured and dependable riding horse. The horse has five gaits, one more than other types of horses.

An old road through the lava flow Eldhraun in South Iceland.

Veiðivötn lakes have formed through volcanic eruptions in centuries past.

Markarfljót river spreads out over the lowlands in South Iceland.
Leirá, a glacial river east of Mýrdalsjökull glacier.

The nature baths by Lake Mývatn in December.

The hamlet Gjögur by Reykjafjörður fjord in the Strandir region. Westfjords.

Horse round-up in Víðidalur valley in North Iceland.
Horse herding in Landeyjar, flatlands west of Eyjafjallajökull glacier.

Dried fish processing in Dalvík village by Eyjafjörður fjord.

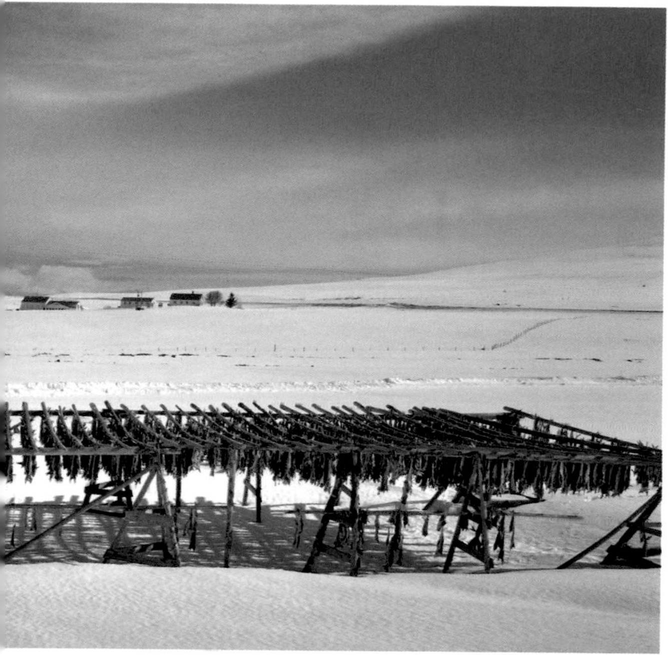

Sheep herding by Lake Mývatn.

Múlajökull, a glacier tongue in the south part of Hofsjökull.
The outlet glacier Gígjökull in Eyjafjallajökull glacier, right
before the 2010 eruption.

The mountain Súlur out from Breiðdalsvík bay in East Iceland.

The lava field from Laki Fires 1783-1784. South Iceland.

Lava columns by Lake Mývatn.
Left page. The church Grundarkirkja in Eyjafjörður fjord was built in 1904.

A track leads through Pokahryggir ridges north to Landmannalaugar.

Mælifellssandur plain north of Mýrdalsjökull glacier.

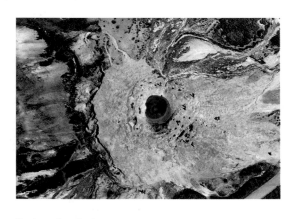

Geysir seen from the air.
The view over the waterfall Gullfoss.

Dyrhólaey promontory is the southernmost point of Iceland.

Jökulgil is a long valley or gorge which stretches from Landmannalaugar up to Torfajökull glacier. A fantastic interplay of forms and colours.

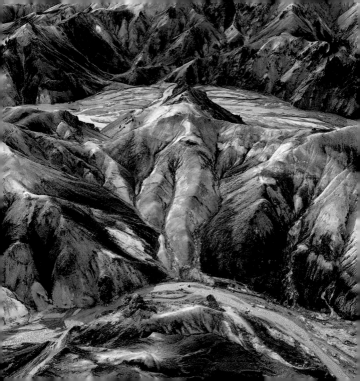

Moss-grown lava in Þingvellir National Park.

Vatnaöldur (Water Dunes) on the way to Landmannalaugar.

Fountain Apple-Moss by the mountain road from South Iceland
north into the highlands.
Seljavallalaug, an old swimming pool. The ground covered with ash from
the eruption in Eyjafjallajökull glacier.

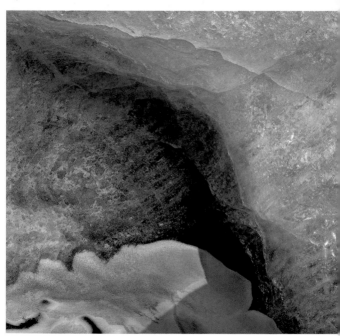

The glacial lake Fjallsárlón south of Vatnajökull glacier.

Seljavallakot farm covered with ash from the 2010 Eyjafjallajökull eruption.
The resulting ash cloud severely disrupted flights around the world.

After the 2010 eruption, the ground near the volcano was covered with ash.

The siblings from the farm Núpstaður west of Lómagnúpur mountain.

The canyon of Markarfljót river is painted red by iron deposits.
Skógafoss waterfall, Eyjafjöll mountains.

The view from Hvestudalur valley into Arnarfjörður fjord in the Westfjords.

Raufarhöfn, Iceland's northernmost village, was once a major fishing town.

Seal hunting at Drangar farm in North Strandir region.
Left page. The Earl of Suðureyri, a fishing village in the Westfjords.

Climbers on Sólheimajökull glacier.

An iceberg on Fjallsárlón glacial lake.

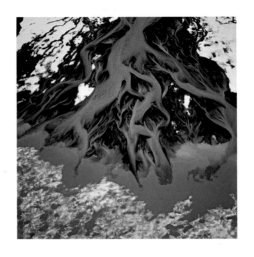

The river Fúlakvísl runs into Hvítárvatn lake by Langjökull glacier.
Hagavatn lake by the roots of Langjökull glacier.

An arch rock by Arnarstapi village on Snæfellsnes peninsula.

Hraunfossar waterfalls run into the river Hvítá in Borgarfjörður fjord.

Stapafell by Arnarstapi on the west part of Snæfellsnes.
A farmer on Snæfellsnes peninsula with newborn lambs.

Foss á Síðu, three farms by Route 1 in South Iceland.

Hveradalir valleys in the Kerlingarfjöll range in the central highlands.

Snæfellsjökull glacier on the outermost part of Snæfellsnes peninsula.

A lake in the highlands by Tungnaá river east of Veiðivötn lakes.
Einhyrningur mountain northwest of Mýrdalsjökull glacier. The view north
into the highlands.

Tungnaá glacial river, a short distance from Landmannalaugar.

Waterfall in Jökulsárgljúfur National Park.
The volcano Hekla and the river Þjórsá.

In Kálfshamarsvík, a columnar basalt inlet in northwest Iceland.

There are several exciting hiking trails around Landmannalaugar.

The Gay Pride parade in Reykjavík is an annual event.
From the centre of Reykjavík.

The old herring town of Siglufjörður is a popular tourist destination.

The view over the shipyard and the old west part of Reykjavík.

Iceland small world

Photographs on front cover and back cover:
House in Hofsós village and Icelandic puffin.

Iceland small world © Sigurgeir Sigurjónsson 2012
2nd edition 2013, 3rd edition 2014
Photographs: © Sigurgeir Sigurjónsson 2012
Foreword: Arni Thorarinsson
Text: Helga J. Gísladóttir
Translation to English: Jónas Ólafsson
Design: Sigurgeir Sigurjónsson
Layout: Jenný Sigurgeirsdóttir
Printed by Prentmiðlun
Publishing and distribution: Portfolio

ISBN 978-9979-72-104-8

Djúpavík in the Strandir region had a busy industry based on herring catches.